CW01216690

Banbury
in old picture postcards

by Ted Clark

European Library ZALTBOMMEL/THE NETHERLANDS

Cover picture:
Queen Victoria's Diamond Jubilee celebration at Banbury was the biggest ever known, surpassing that of the Golden Jubilee of her accession. The 'Red Lion' Hotel is seen here gaily decorated for the occasion. The Hotel was demolished in 1930 to make way for Woolworth's Store.

GB ISBN 90 288 2037 X

© 1982 European Library – Zaltbommel/The Netherlands

Third edition, 1996: reprint of the original edition of 1982.

No part of this book may be reproduced in any form, by print, photoprint, microfilm or any other means, without written permission from the publisher.

INTRODUCTION

Banbury is a fascinating town. To the newcomer it may seem to be modern with its busy streets and industrial and housing estates, but its history goes back no less than 1,500 years. Equally interesting are the surrounding villages, all linked to the town at the centre throughout the 19th century by carriers' carts. Today the carrier's cart is no more, but the natural link remains.

Banbury began when Saxon invaders from the Wash founded two settlements on the river Cherwell. One they named Banbury and the other Grimsbury. During the Saxon period Banbury grew, engulfing Wykham where there had been a Roman villa, while Grimsbury remained almost static. The Saxons of the settlements were pagan, but in 634 Bishop Birinus converted the West Saxons to Christianity and King Cynegils was baptised at Dorchester-on-Thames. The King appointed the Bishop to the see of Dorchester and included Banbury in it.

The Saxons had approached Banbury using the Banbury Lane from Northampton. Some three hundred years later the Danes at Northampton broke the truce and using the same line of approach pillaged and plundered their way to Banbury and North Oxfordshire. A battle to save the town was fought at Danesmoor but in all probability Banbury was left in ruins.

However, the Danes were keen traders. They introduced new trade and laid out the Market Place in the form it is today. Banbury suffered further devastation as the result of the struggle among Saxon earls. The Norman conquest occurred the next year 1066. The Normans left a far deeper impression on the town because it was Bishop Alexander, Bishop of Lincoln, where the see was transferred in 1070, who started to build the cathedral-like church, which was later referred to as 'the glory of Banbury'. He also built a great castle, which dominated the Market Place, and brought much trade and pageantry when it was visited by Kings, Bishop and Lords. The castle was also reputed to be a 'terrible' prison and during the period of religious persecution, in the 16th century, Recusants were confined there and at Broughton Castle.

Banbury's first town charter was granted by Queen Mary on January 24th, 1554 and one of the first things the new council did was to remove the punitive equipment, wooden cage, stocks, pillory and ducking stool to the Town Hall in Cornhill, although the castle continued as a gaol for some years.

In the latter years of Elizabeth 1st reign Banbury had become widely known as a hot-bed Puritanism. Its Member of Parliament, Sir Anthony Cope, of Hanwell Castle, was the leader in Parliament, locally sermons were preached with passion and the frenzied iconoclasts damaged the parish church and in 1600 destroyed the Cross which had become known throughout the world in connection with the nursery rhyme. The rectitude of Banbury became synonymous with Puritanism in London and elsewhere.

In the first half of the 17th century two disasters befell the town. The first was the great fire of 1628 which started in Calthorpe Lane while many were in church and, spreading, destroyed hundreds of houses, twenty malt kilns and several granaries. Then in 1642 occurred the Civil War. Banbury was strongly Parliamentarian but the castle was held for the King and there was much hard fighting. Twice the castle was beseiged. The church was the headquarters of the Parliamentary troops and was badly damaged as were many houses in the Market Place and others were destroyed altogether. After the war Parliament granted materials for reconstruction and bought the castle from Lord Saye and Sele. It was dismantled and the stones given to the people to repair their houses.

Although Banbury cakes had for long been known they reached famous proportions when made by Betty White and her husband Jarvis. Others followed including Mrs. E.W. Brown in the same premises and the Bett family in the High Street. Banbury was also famous in the 18th and 19th centuries for weaving and for plush which it supplied to the Houses of Parliament and many royal houses throughout Europe and local machines also made livery for servants at Windsor Castle.

The original Banbury Cross, as related, was destroyed as a result of Puritan zeal in 1600 and the town lost its castle when it was demolished at the end of the Civil War. In 1790 its cathedral-like church, begun by Bishop Alexander and added to by later generations, suffered the same fate, needlessly it is now thought. It was undoubtedly in need of major repair as the result of war and neglect. The present church, on the same site, replaced the former church in 1797 although the tower was not added until 22 years later.

The new Banbury Cross was erected in 1859 although the statues were not added until 1914. It is hoped that the following pages will remind those who knew the town sixty years ago and more of those days and that they will vividly portray to the younger generation their most interesting heritage.

The author is particularly grateful to the following who allowed him to make a choice from their collections of old postcards for use in this book: Mrs. L.W. Brummitt, Mrs. Winifred Johnson, Mrs. Sheila Stewart and Mrs. Viggers, of Banbury, Mr. Michael Bennett, of Enstone, Mr. Jack Honey, of Middleton Cheney, Mr. Ron Linford, of Adderbury, Mr. George Walker, of Alcan and Lord Saye and Sele, of Broughton Castle. He is also grateful for photographic help received from Mr. Iain Buchanan, chief photographer of 'The Banbury Guardian'.

1. The very centre of Queen Victoria's Diamond Jubilee celebrations in 1897 was the Jubilee fete on the Horse Fair. First a feu de joie was fired there by the Volunteers, a thanksgiving service was held at St. Mary's Church and a procession, which took one and a half hours to pass, paraded the town. Flags and bunting streamed out everywhere, illuminations coloured the occasion at night and finally a bonfire was lit on Crouch Hill at 10 p.m.

2. The highly decorated High Street on Diamond Jubilee day; the placard across the street reads 'Victoria's reign, grand great and glorious' and Mr. Stanley's shop, later occupied by Frdk W. Ginger and now Frdk Anker, bore the initials V.R. proudly. The former Conservative Club, left, was lit at night by four hundred lamps in celebration.

3. A street scene in Grimsbury on Diamond Jubilee day. A report states: *In Grimsbury there were evident signs of rejoicing,... ...in Middleton Road streamers reaching from the palisading in front to the windows on the second floor. There was hardly a house without some sort of decoration.*

4. A Post Office telegraph machine started to operate in the town in the 1890's. This 'demonstration' of the 'new wonder' was given to the public on Diamond Jubilee day. The man in the bowler hat and with buttonhole, would appear to be the proud manager of the local exchange.

> IN COMMEMORATION OF THE
> Diamond Jubilee of Queen Victoria,
> 1837-1897.
>
> A NEW CLOCK WITH WESTMINSTER QUARTERS, THREE ADDITIONAL BELLS, AND THE CHIMES PLAYING 21 TUNES, WERE PLACED IN THE TOWER, AND THE PEAL OF BELLS RETUNED, BY PUBLIC SUBSCRIPTION.
>
> C. F. PORTER, VICAR.
> W. LAKE, MAYOR.
> W. POTTS, SECRETARY.
>
> JUNE 22, 1897.

5. The more permanent reminder of Diamond Jubilee day was the installation and starting of a new clock at St. Mary's Church with three additional bells and chimes. However all nearly went wrong for at midnight on June 21st, the day before the celebrations, the installation was not complete and all through the night workmen toiled. However at noon on June 22nd, the Mayor cut the ribbon, the clock played the hour chime and struck twelve. The day was saved.

Carriers Parade, Banbury.

6. Throughout the 19th century the Carrier's Cart was the connecting link between village and town. In the middle years of the century there were 208 Carriers paying 465 visits a week. In 1914, however, only 118 were doing so, paying 292 visits a week. This decline was due to the opening of the railways and the development of the postal services. Great pride was taken in turnout and appearance of the carts as typified in the picture.

The Sheep Market, Banbury.

7. The wool trade was an important one for Banbury from the Middle Ages to the 19th century. In the earliest days the western end of High Street was known as Sheep Street and there was a Wool Hall there. In various parts of the town there was a beast market, a hog market, a corn market (Cornhill) and a horse market. Sheep were sold on the eastern side of the Horse Fair until Midland Marts opened their market in 1931.

8. The north side of the Horse Fair was occupied by elegant private houses before St. Mary's Church acquired the site in 1904 to build the Church House to cope with the increasing need for social activities. Church House was opened in 1905, the last year of Canon Porter's incumbency.

9. ...the scene just after the Church House was built. For seventy years it played a most important part in the social life of the town — plays, concerts, dances, whist drives being held there, in addition to church meetings. In recent years it has been replaced by St. Mary's Centre.

10. Originally the interior of St. Mary's Church was colour washed and far more austere than the elaborate interior known to later generations. In 1858 an eastern gallery was removed and the chancel, which did not extend to the height of the church, opened to the view of the people. The postcard is of the church's interior in 1910.

11. Onlookers crowd round the members of the Warwickshire Hunt when they meet at Banbury Cross on February 15th, 1907. The majority of the men wears caps and the women tie their bonnets on securely under the chin. Meets of hounds at the Cross were always popular, particularly on Boxing Day morning.

12. Removal of a lime tree on the corner of The Green and South Bar after a gale had blown the top off the tree. The tree must have been in a dangerous state for some time as bricks have been used to fill the hollow in the trunk of the tree. The occurance would have been after 1901.

13. Horse and master slowly trot their way along West Bar in 1915. The scene has not greatly changed except that most of the properties on the left were then in private hands. At the end of the street a delivery is being made by horse-drawn transport.

14. The top of High Street in 1908. The boys wear knickerbockers, the delivery man with sackcart has a peaked cap and a dray is drawn across the road to facilitate delivery. On the left is the 'George and Dragon' public house and in the far distance can be seen the former premises of the Conservative Club.

15. Lower down the High Street in 1908. The pony trap stands outside S.H. Jones' shop which later moved to the other side of the road. There is no large clock as yet above the pavement where the road narrows. This was to come when Frdk W. Ginger opened his clockmaking premises there.

16. The ancient coaching inn on the right is the 'Red Lion', which was demolished in 1930 to make way for Woolworths' Store. It was not only a coaching inn in its time but the Post Office. Most of the important town dinners were held in the dining room, for example the inaugural dinner for the Mayor each November.

17. The saloon bar of the 'Red Lion' frequented by leading business men and farmers. Its main window looked directly onto the High Street and entry to it was through the yard. The posters are advertising the programme at the Palace Cinema — Ronald Coleman starring as 'Bulldog Drummond'.

18. The yard of the 'Red Lion', which was always presented an animated scene on Thursdays when corn dealers set up their stands on either side and Second Edition copies of 'The Banbury Guardian' were sold at the main doorway. Inside are hung the latest railway timetables. 'The Guardian's' second edition contained the day's market report.

19. An advertisement card for Betts' 'celebrated Banbury Cakes by parcel post'. Seven cakes could be bought for 1s 6d — today's equivalent $7\frac{1}{2}$p. The card depicts the scene before 1900 because the full statue of Ceres still surmounts the Corn Exchange.

20. The old houses in the High Street about 1909. Betts have been appointed suppliers of Banbury Cakes to the Royal household and the Royal coat of arms is proudly displayed. Neale and Perkins, the ironmongers, occupy the other part of the building, displaying their wares at the roadside.

HIGH STREET, BANBURY, ON MARKET DAY.

21. The Thursday market day scene in 1902 in the lower half of High Street leading into the Cow Fair. The inn on the left is the 'Catherine Wheel'. Railings have been erected to keep the cattle from pushing over the footpath. The sides leading from path to roadway are grooved to take cattle urine into the drains. The cattle went from the streets in 1931, when after Midland Marts opened their saleyard.

22. Animated scene in May 1910 when the Mayor, Mr. H.F.R. Brooks, proclaims the reign of George Vth, to the people. The dais is occupied by councillors and officials; the balcony above mostly by councillor's wives. Note the ornamental gas lamps, Lamprey's shop and boys in the forefront of the picture in Eton collars.

23. The not-very-busy scene at Banbury Town Hall at 11:30 a.m. on a Thursday market day in summer. Cattle are being controlled by drovers on the left. The Midland Red bus is dropping its passengers. Buses started and finished their journeys here many years after the picture was taken.

24. Banbury Market Place on a summer's day in 1907. There are as yet few trading stalls. Carriers' carts line the roadway and agricultural machinery is displayed in front of Broughton and Wilks' shop. The ornamental gas standard in the foreground was removed long since.

25. A view of the Market Place looking West about 1907. The stalls are not ready for business. Pigs are penned in the foreground awaiting buyers. Two well-known shops can be seen, Nathans Domestic Stores on the left middle ground and top left, Robin's Bros'. Tudor premises, which, when restored in recent years, revealed shots fired in the Civil War embedded in its pargetted front.

26. A 1930 view of Cornhill when the Vine public house, originally one of two corn exchanges built as rivals in 1857, was in its heyday. St. John Ambulance Brigade has taken over the building in the centre, occupied first by Gilletts Bank, later Barclays. Banbury's first Cross was in Cornhill and its first Town Hall there also.

27. The Banbury Great Western Railway station as it was known to travellers by train until well after the Second World War. A new station was built only after prolonged pressure. The London North Western Railway (later London Midland & Scottish) was the first to make a connection (followed by the Great Central). Banbury had two stations, one on either side of the bridge.

28. The Original Cake Shop while in the occupation of E.W. Brown in Parson's Street. The firm provided a restaurant service and daily baked bread. It was from these premises that Betty White sold and made a name for the cakes. In 1967 the shop was sold to developers. Before a preservation order had been placed on it they began to demolish it. Representations were made, but too late for the building to be preserved.

29. The wistaria tree at Brown's Cake Shop which was only equalled in length and beauty by that at the 'White Lion' Hotel, which has happily been preserved as the result of great care during alterations in recent years.

30. Banbury's only surviving Tudor public house, the Reindeer in Parson's Street, as it was in 1918. Carved on its massive yard doors and dated 1570 are the names of John Knight and David Horn, the latter probably the innkeeper. John Knight was a baker and owned much property in Elizabethan times and the family was an important one. Royalist sympathisers were executed in the yard of the inn in the Civil War.

31. The Globe Room at the Reindeer Inn was an extension to the inn and built in 1637. The Civil War picture 'When did you last see your father?' had this room as a background. The panelling of the room was sold and 'lost' for over fifty years but in 1964 its whereabouts was discovered and it was bought back by the town. It is now to be seen again at the inn.

North Bar and St. Mary's Church, Banbury.

32. North Bar as it appeared in 1905. On the left of the picture, immediately beyond the lampost, can be seen the doorway to the former home of the Bolton family, who carried on the wool trade for many years and was the last of the four principal firms to do so. The house has a panelled oak room dating back to 1641. The premises are now occupied by a firm of solicitors.

33. Christ Church, South Banbury, in Broad Street, which was in existence for 114 years. It was opened in 1853 to cope with the increase in population in that area of the town, but with the decline in the mid-twentieth century it was merged with St. Mary's. When planned it was to have a spire but this was never added.

34. The interior of Christ Church which had a seating capacity of seven hundred. The reredos was in Caen stone and among the memorial windows was one to His Royal Highness the Prince Consort, the cost of which was defrayed by public subscription.

WESLEYAN CHAPEL & MARLBOROUGH ROAD BANBURY.

35. The Methodist Church in Marlborough Road. The first Methodist Church was on South Bar and the second in Church Lane. When Dr. Stanton Wise developed the Beech Lawn estate in 1853 and Marlborough Road was cut through to the High Street, the Methodists bought a site for their third church on it. It was opened on May 9th, 1865.

36. The imposing premises in Marlborough Road. The building to the right (with the scroll at the top) was built and given by Sir Bernhard Samuelson, the ironmaster, as a Mechanics Institute for the benefit of his workpeople. All the science and art classes in the town were moved there. For many years the building has operated as the town's library. In 1893, largely owing to Sir Bernhard, the building to the left was opened as a Secondary and Technical School under the title of the Municipal School, the forerunner to Banbury School. The school's playing field was in Grimsbury.

Broad Street, Banbury

37. Broad Stret as it appeared in 1908. It contained an extensive row of Banbury Co-operative & Industrial Society shops and their flour mill. Beyond the church can be seen thatched cottages and beyond them cattle railings to confine cattle when the Cow Fair proved too small to contain all the stock brought in for sale. The inn on the right is believed to have been 'The Volunteer'.

38. An advertisement postcard issued by the Banbury Co-operative Society to mark the opening of their tailor's shop in August 1908. The figures quoted on the card are interesting. For the half-year 1866, when the Society started, membership was 88 and sales £396. In June 1908 the figures were 3,254 members and sales £102,420.

39. In the early 19th century Roman Catholics worshipped in a chapel at Overthorpe following which a mission was started in the lower narrow part of High Street. Dr. Tandy, in charge of the mission, who was reputedly a friend of Pugin, the famous architect, brought the new church in South Bar into being in 1838, a plot of land being bought for its erection from the Calthorpe estate.

St. John's Church, Banbury

Horton Infirmary, Banbury

40. The Horton Infirmary when still very much a cottage hospital. It is named after Miss Horton, of Middleton Cheney, whose intention was to give money to build a hospital, but who died before it was carried out. Her nephew, a beneficiary of her will, provided the necessary capital. It was opened on July 17th, 1872. The advent of two world wars and a greatly increased population has led to a vast increase in its size and scope.

41. St. Leonard's Church, Grimsbury, built as a chapel of ease to Christ Church in 1891, came into being, like its mother church, as a result of the Oxford Movement. Ironically the daughter church flourishes while the mother church has been demolished. This situation was brought about by the movement of population, the growth of Grimsbury and the newer estates on the outskirts of the town to the south and west. The rondels in the church, depicting the Stations of the Cross, were formerly in Christ Church.

42. A picture taken about 1870 of Bernhard Samuelson and some of his workforce. Apart from Mr. Samuelson (as he then was), in the centre, the only name known is Mr. Gardiner, a brother of Mrs. Betts, the cake maker, who sits behind the boy on the low stool in the front row. Samuelson's started in 1846, made and exported agricultural machining all over the world. It turned Banbury from a market town into an industrial one.

FIRE AT SAMUELSONS   OCT 18TH 1912

43. A postcard was published in October 1912 to record the great fire at the Lower Britannia Works of Samuelson's in the early hours of Friday, October 18th. Three long 'shops' about 250 feet in length were completely destroyed together with milling machinery ready for exporting to South Africa. It was the biggest fire Banbury had witnessed for years and thousands went to see the gutted workshops.

44. Workers break down hand grenades at one of the two shell filling factories established near the Overthorpe Road during the 1914-1918 World War. After the war thousands of tons equipment was broken down. There was only one fatality at the factories in the war years.

45. The machine room at Cheney and Sons printing works in Calthorpe Street after the fire on Wednesday, March 14th, 1923 which, in half an hour, destroyed the whole of the plant as well as the paper and ink stock. The roofs of three of the four bays fell in. However most of the composing room was saved and with the help of other local firms and the use of the nearby Drill Hall work was continued. New and extended works were opened in November of the same year.

The Car after Accident, June 10th, 1907, in which two American ladies and two gentlemen were travelling. All were badly injured, one gentleman succumbed three hours after accident.

46. Sunrising Hill, on the Banbury to Stratford-upon-Avon road, was the scene of many accidents in the early years of the century. It was much feared. Brakes often gave way and drivers lost control. Postcards were issued to record these unhappy events. The car above had been carrying American visitors.

Place marked X exact spot where accident occurred, June 10th, 1907.

47. ...the tree at the sharp bend half way down the hill seemed to draw cars towards it. This card records the exact sport of collision.

48. ...a showman's vehicle being recovered after it had crashed on Sunrising Hill in 1910. The vehicle had, apparently, been carrying animals for show.

49. Banbury Cross in 1920 — the age of popular motoring was about to begin. The Cross is fully equipped with statues and railings and lamps protect it. A bull-nosed Morris car receives attention at the garage on the right.

50. South Bar, the road into the town from Oxford, always presents a refreshing appearance. The addition of St. John's Church and later the lime trees in 1885 enhanced its looks. Today its impressive width is obscured by cars parked on either side of the roadway.

51. Today, with the vast volume of traffic passing Banbury Cross, it is almost unbelievable that in 1920 it was not necessary to keep to the left of the Cross. A Midland Red bus can be seen passing to the right of the Cross to enter High Street.

52. The Waits which heralded the dawn of Christmas Day by playing seasonal music around the centre of the town. They were a part of The Minstrels who from the early 1900's frequently gave concerts near the Town Hall or on South Bar near the Cross in summertime. They were led by George Hutchings in the centre. The Waits ceased to play in 1939.

53. The original sheet mill building at the Northern Aluminium Company's works in 1931. A second was added in 1938. The coming of the firm to the town boosted employment prospects and brought in many newcomers.

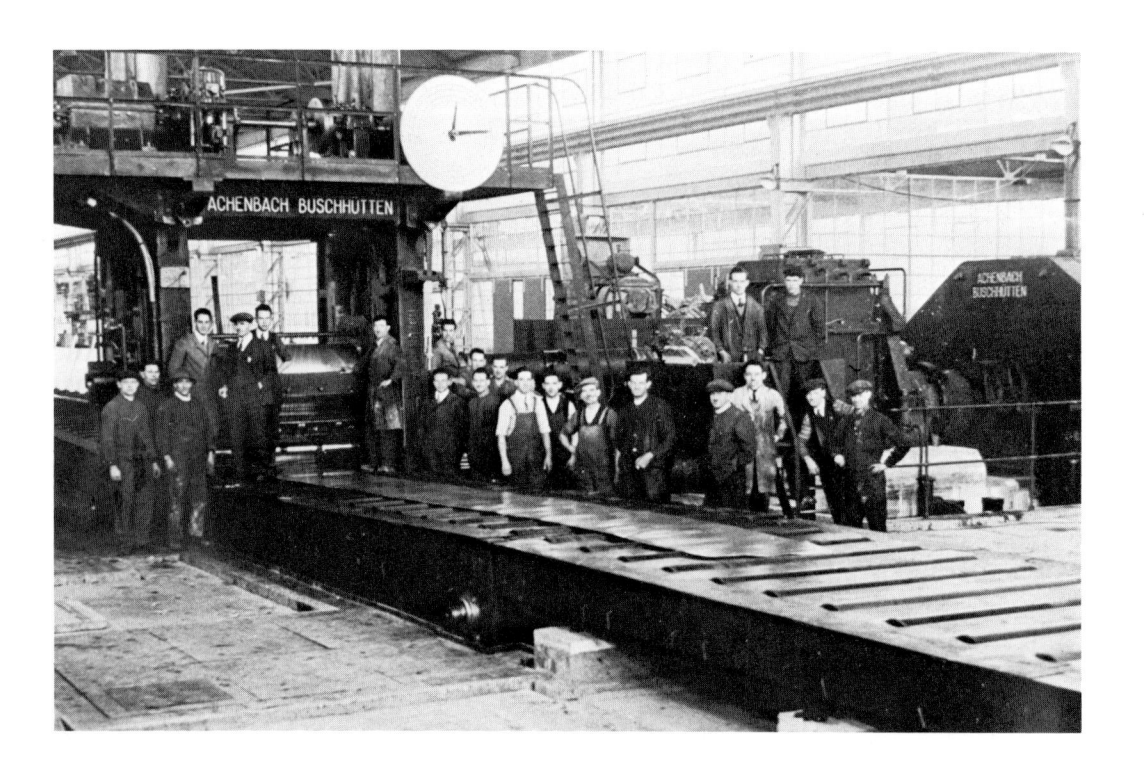

54. Final adjustments being made to the first hot aluminium rolling mill at the Northern Aluminium Company's works in October 1931. The mill started a month later.

55. The bells of St. Mary's, Banbury, being returned to the tower on April 3rd, 1930 after being recast with a ringing peal of ten bells, with two others giving half-notes for the chimes (sadly now not in use) but not in the peal. The Bagleys, of Chacombe, cast six bells for the original church, two more being added in 1820. Except in the case of one bell, all the old metal was re-used and the original inscription preserved. The oldest bell has the inscription 'I ring to Sermon with a lusty Boome, that all may come and none may stay at home'.

56. A float of the Wilts United Dairies Ltd. prepared and ready for a Workpeople's Hospital Association carnival and fete about 1924. The event was held annually until 1939 and on it the hospital relied greatly for funds and also on the army of volunteer collectors who made weekly collections. Note the cheese presses at the rear of the vehicle and the lack of windscreen and oil lamps. The driver is George Collins.

57. The coat of arms of the Borough of Banbury which did duty until 1951 when, because the 'Sun in Glory' had never been properly registered, a new coat of arms was prepared. The motto 'God is our sun and shield' has, happily, been continued. It seems likely that this originated from the daily reading of the Psalter at Lincoln Cathedral by the Rector of Banbury as far back as Norman times.

58. Broughton Castle with its moat and dramatic associations with the struggle against Charles I has always attracted many visitors. This postcard picture shows ivy on the wall, indicative of the 1890's.

59. The Great Hall of Broughton Castle as it was in the late 19th and early 20th century, when Col. Lord Algernon Gordon Lennox occupied it and who, at that time, occasionally opened it to the public. Local people used to travel out to it by horse brake. The armour in the Great Hall today still occupies the same niches.

60. Lady Gordon-Lennox's bedroom at the time she and her husband occupied the Castle. In Victorian fashion, all rooms were filled with furniture. As Prince of Wales, Edward VII paid a visit to the house shortly before he ascended the throne in 1901.

Wroxton Abbey, Banbury

61. Wroxton Abbey, about 1890 when, at that time, it was fashionable to have ivy overgrowing the walls. The house's most famous occupant was Lord North, Prime Minister, during the War of American Independence. He was elected member of Parliament for Banbury thirteen times. Today the house is in the occupation of an American University and much money has been spent on restoring it.

EDGEHILLS, near Banbury, where the famous battle was fought between the armies of Cromwell and Charles I., on Sunday morning, October 23rd, 1642.

62. The tower at Edgehill, the point where, it is said, Charles I viewed the battlefield of 1642. The tower itself was not built until over hundred years later and it was then done so as a place where Sanderson Miller, of Radway, could entertain his friends. The design is from Guy's Tower at Warwick Castle. The original entrance was by drawbridge from the smaller tower.

63. A turn-of-the-century postcard of Sulgrave Manor, six miles from Banbury, which was built in the 16th century by Lawrence Washington, the great-great-grandfather of George Washington, the 'father' of the United States and its first President. It was given to the people of the United States by British people in 1914 to mark the centenary of peace between the two nations which began with the Treaty of Ghent in 1812. It was restored and refurnished by joint British and American effort in 1924. It is interesting that both Lord North, Prime Minister and General George Washington, at the time of the War of American Independence, had close associations with this part of England.

The Green, Adderbury.

64. The Green at Adderbury, on which Morris Men still love to dance, is surrounded by magnificent houses, notably the 17th century one where Lord Montague, William III's minister, lived and Adderbury House, once the home of the poet, John Wilmot, Earl of Rochester and afterwards of the second Duke of Argyll. The magnificent 15th century church befits a large town rather than a village. The armorial bearings and bust of William of Wykham, for whom the church was built, are to be seen in the chancel roof. The Rev. Christopher Rawlins founded a grammar school in the village in 1554 and the present Primary School is named after him.

Bloxham Village.

The Morland Series — *Produced in Banbury*

65. The street scene at Bloxham in 1905. On the left, part of All Saint's School, founded by the Rev. P.R. Egerto and now run in connection with the Woodard Corporation. The church spire of St. Mary, rhymed for its length (195 feet), towers overall. The slender spire, because of its length, does not get the praise its beauty warrants.

66. The High Street at Deddington in the early 20th century. Note the rough state of the road -the main road to Oxford- and the lack of drains to carry away surface water. Charles I slept in the village before the battle of Cropredy Bridge in 1644. The tower of the church had fallen down in 1634 and he noticed that the bells could be made into cannon balls. He had them sent to New College for this purpose promising in the future to 'restore same in material or monies'. When the church was rebuilt it was done in impressive style.

67. Securities were sold by the Government in both the First and Second World Wars to provide the necessary arms and ammunition to prosecute the wars. This shell was presented to the people of Deddington to commemorate their notable efforts in this connection during guns week in 1918.

HIGH STREET, HOOK NORTON.

PHOTO BY A. W. WHEELER.
PRODUCED BY B. R. MORLAND, BANBURY.
Sold by J. Spatcher, Hook Norton.

68. The centre of Hook Norton in 1911 with the Union Jack flying bravely from the tower of St. Peter's, parts of which date back to the Saxons. Until the Second World War the greatest village event was St. Peter's Day when as many as two hundred sat down to a tea and entertainment. Miss Margaret Dickens was responsible for the event for many years and for much social activity. A plaque in her memory is in the church and a bell has been dedicated to her. Hook Norton possesses a flourishing brewery one of the few village breweries to survive in recent years. It was started in a farmhouse 133 years ago.

69. The old Elm tree at Upper Tysoe, a landmark for generations, had to be felled in the Spring of 1978 as it was being badly weakened by elm disease. For many years children had been able to climb into the bowl of the tree and upwards as it was so hollow.

THE GREEN, MIDDLETON CHENEY

70. Middle Green, Middleton Cheney, when the power unit on the farm was the horse and not the tractor. The haywain is loaded and awaiting its collection on the morrow. The Green has always been owned by the Squire. Middleton's 14th century church, with 150 feet spire rising from its eight pinnacled tower, has no less than eight pre-Raphaelite windows from the William Morris workshop, the reason being that a former Rector was a friend of Sir Edward Burne-Jones. Near the west door of the church are the graves of Roundheads who died in the battle of Middleton in 1643.

71. Mr. Harry Bonham, in the centre of the group, with his carrier's cart which plied from Middleton Cheney for many years. He was also a prominent personality in local government affairs. The card was published when he won the 'best turn out' prize at the annual carriers' parade. With him are some of his customers.

Horley, near Banbury.

72. The lovely village of Horley, nestling on the southern slopes of the hills, as seen from the Wroxton road in 1906. For many years there was no easy access to the village and it must have been self-supporting. However by 1906 the Mill (second building on the left) had finished functioning although the flow of water is as strong as ever. The building immediately behind on the hillside was used from 1915 to 1930 to house children in the care of the Banbury Board of Guardians, which proved to be a happy arrangement. Horley church possesses one of the largest and finest paintings on its north wall of St. Christopher crossing a stream with the young Christ on his shoulder.

73. 'Old' Mr. Walton and Postman Franklin chat outside the Post Office at Wardington in the early years of the century. Postman Franklin lived at Middleton Cheney. He walked to Banbury to collect the mail and delivered it in Wardington and Chipping Warden before walking home.

74. For over one hundred years the editorship of The Banbury Guardian was in the hands of the Potts family. At first the paper appeared monthly as 'The Guardian' under the first William Potts in 1838. Five years later 'The Banbury Guardian', a weekly publication, made its bow. John Potts succeeded his father in 1867 and for a short time published 'The Banbury Evening News' when he quarrelled with the post office over posting news telegrams on the office windows. His son, William, the last of the trio, was editor for fifty-five years until his death in 1947.

75. Ten thousand people attended Aviation Day held on a field in Warwick Road on April 26th, 1932. Five light planes and a three engined airliner were shown by Sir Alan Cobham (centre) seen with the Mayor (Mr. W.T. Palmer) and Lady Cobham. A draw for flights was made at the Palace Cinema on the night previous. Members of the town council, representatives of other bodies and the Press, were taken up for trips in the airliner in groups of ten.

76. One of the most unusual characters to live in the Banbury area for many generations was Theodore Lamb who for nearly forty years lived as a hermit in a crudely constructed shack beside the Banbury to Shipston road at Sibford. He lived frugally and wore sackcloth. He maintained himself by repairing clocks and watches for which he had been trained. He was scrupulously honest although his ragged appearance was frightening. He rode a bicycle without rubber tyres and drew a trolley at the back filled with pots and pans. His self-inflicted solitude closed with his death from pneumonia aged seventy.